Careers in
ENGINEERING

A Career In Civil Engineering

D1264764

Other titles in the *Careers in Engineering* series include:

A Career in Biomedical Engineering
A Career in Computer Engineering
A Career in Electrical Engineering
A Career in Environmental Engineering
A Career in Mechanical Engineering

Careers in
ENGINEERING

A Career In
Civil
Engineering

James Roland

ReferencePoint
Press®

San Diego, CA

© 2019 ReferencePoint Press, Inc.
Printed in the United States

For more information, contact:
ReferencePoint Press, Inc.
PO Box 27779
San Diego, CA 92198
www.ReferencePointPress.com

ALL RIGHTS RESERVED.
No part of this work covered by the copyright hereon may be reproduced or used in any form or by any means—graphic, electronic, or mechanical, including photocopying, recording, taping, web distribution, or information storage retrieval systems—without the written permission of the publisher.

LIBRARY OF CONGRESS CATALOGING-IN-PUBLICATION DATA

Name: Roland, James, author.
Title: A Career in Civil Engineering/by James Roland.
Description: San Diego, CA: ReferencePoint Press, Inc., 2019. | Series: Careers in Engineering | Includes bibliographical references and index. | Audience: Grades 9 to 12.
Identifiers: LCCN 2017060395 (print) | LCCN 2018000698 (ebook) | ISBN 9781682823460 (eBook) | ISBN 9781682823453 (hardback)
Subjects: LCSH: Civil engineering—Vocational guidance—Juvenile literature.
Classification: LCC TA157 (ebook) | LCC TA157 .R64128 2019 (print) | DDC 624.023—dc23
LC record available at https://lccn.loc.gov/2017060395

CONTENTS

CIVIL ENGINEER AT A GLANCE

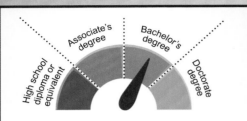

Educational Requirements
Bachelor's degree and above

Certification and Licensing

Fundamentals of engineering exam and professional engineer license (required)

Working Conditions

Inside

Outside

Personal Qualities

- ☑ Strong math and science skills
- ☑ Problem-solving skills
- ☑ Able to work both independently and with a team

Median pay in 2016   **$83,540**

303,500

Number of jobs as of 2016

Growth rate through 2026

11%

Future Job Outlook

Source: Bureau of Labor Statistics, *Occupational Outlook Handbook*. www.bls.gov.

Building the World We Live In

The undersea tunnel that connects France with England was one of the greatest construction challenges of the last century. The Chunnel, as it is known, carries trains, cars, and trucks between the European continent and the island that is home to England, Scotland, and Wales. What makes this possible is an underwater tunnel that is 32 miles (51 km) long and, in some places, about 250 feet (76 m) deep.

Civil engineers were key to making this happen. It was their job to determine where to locate the tunnel, how big around it needed to be, which materials to use, what equipment could get the job done, and how hundreds of workers could safely work underground each day. Working together with dozens of other engineers (and other construction professionals) the civil engineers helped build this magnificent structure—which opened in 1994 and is still very much in use today.

The Built Environment

Civil engineering is a field of engineering that is specifically concerned with the built environment, or the things that are designed and constructed for human activity. Civil engineers are involved with the planning and building of skyscrapers, water and sewer systems, highways, bridges, tunnels, airports, marinas, and other big projects used by lots of people. Civil engineers also work on smaller projects, such as planning a network of bicycle paths or designing a new type of tugboat to move ships around in a harbor.

They are responsible for designing, building, and maintaining the infrastructure that supports modern civilizations. This includes the neighborhoods where people live; the offices, factories, and other places where they work; and the transportation systems that make it possible for people to travel from place to place. Most people interact with the work of a civil engineer at some point every day.

British engineer John Smeaton coined the term *civil engineering* during the eighteenth century. He studied lighthouses and machines and found ways to improve them. He designed new construction methods for lighthouses to better withstand the pounding of waves against their walls. He reconfigured steam engines to make them more powerful. He used the phrase *civil engineering* to distinguish civilian engineers from engineers who designed and built forts, warships, weapons, and other military works. Civil engineering is considered the oldest type of engineering. Today, civil engineers work for the military, for governments, and in the private sector. But modern civil engineers are not all that different from Smeaton himself. They figure out how buildings can last longer, how highways can accommodate more cars, and how machines can work more efficiently, and they develop the ways to turn their visions into realities.

Dream It, Build It

Civil engineering encompasses many complex and challenging areas, but it can be simplified to two basic concepts: design and construction. The design phase of any project begins with a goal and a vision. It is the job of the civil engineer to turn that goal and vision into reality. They must be able to look at an unused piece of land around an airport, for example, and devise a way to add a new terminal or more runways. The civil engineers on the Chunnel project, for instance, started with a gray stretch of choppy water in the North Atlantic. They had to draw up the designs for a tunnel pushing through the bedrock under the water and have every detail anticipated before work crews arrived.

Construction begins once a design is approved and government permits have been obtained. A civil engineering construction project can include brand-new structures or machines as well as additions, repairs, or renovations of existing structures. When a highway needs more lanes because traffic is too congested, a civil engineer figures out how to add more lanes to the existing road. That same civil engineer, or another engineer serving as the project manager, will oversee the construction of those new lanes.

Some civil engineers focus on either design or construction. However, many split their time between the two responsibilities, which means they work both inside at a computer and outside at construction sites. Those construction sites can be in a shipyard, a factory, an oil rig, or a tunnel, on a beach or mountain, or anywhere people are living and working. Civil engineers also work in conjunction with architects, urban planners, business owners, construction workers, and other types of engineers, such as mechanical or electrical engineers. The civil engineer is often the project manager on a job, which means being in charge of contractors and others working on the project. Understanding contracts, budgets, and other aspects of the business side of civil engineering is also important.

"We have water systems at capacity and urban transportation systems falling apart. The network that makes societies work is starting to fall apart. That is where civil and environmental engineers fit."[1]

—James Hunt, a professor of environmental engineering at the University of California, Berkeley

For people who want to design and build projects that can be seen and used by many people, civil engineering offers a wide range of opportunities. The work of civil engineers orbits Earth in the International Space Station and runs underground carrying water, oil, and electricity to people around the world. And everywhere in between are countless examples of civil engineering helping people work, move, and live every day.

Projects Big and Small

But civil engineering is not just about designing and building major construction projects that can be seen by everyone. Civil engineers also improve drainage in a neighborhood that is prone to flooding. They advise oil companies about safe places to drill. They design the engines for mighty ships and help keep them sailing smoothly. They design and oversee construction of seawalls and sand renourishment projects. They are even at the cutting edge of engineering and science, developing new plastics and other materials that will revolutionize construction of the buildings and vehicles of the future.

Civil engineers are hard at work everywhere around the world. There are more than three hundred thousand civil engineers in the United States alone, and annual job growth is in the double digits. The world is moving and changing quickly, and structures and machines are needed to keep up with it all. Small towns and big cities employ civil engineers to help keep traffic moving smoothly. Huge multinational civil engineering firms employ them to build modern cities and rebuild aging infrastructure. "We have water systems at capacity and urban transportation systems falling apart. The network that makes societies work is starting to fall apart," says James Hunt, a professor of environmental engineering at the University of California, Berkeley. "That is where civil and environmental engineers fit."[1]

CHAPTER 1

What Does a Civil Engineer Do?

Civil engineers design, build, supervise, operate, and maintain construction projects and systems. They are also involved in creating and managing budgets for projects and for getting the necessary permits to build the structures and systems. Civil engineers who focus more on design will spend a lot of time in meetings with clients, architects, and government agencies. Civil engineers who focus more on construction will spend a lot of time at the site, working with contractors and subcontractors. Both types of work are rewarding.

A 2017 survey of members of the American Society of Civil Engineers (ASCE) found that civil engineers are generally happy with their salaries and the work they do. The Bureau of Labor Statistics reports that the median annual salary for civil engineers in 2016 was more than $80,000. More experienced engineers and those who are in supervisory roles in large firms can expect to make well into six figures. They are also encouraged about the future of their profession. "It's an exciting time to be a civil engineer," says longtime engineer and engineering professor Norma Jean Mattei, president of the ASCE, adding,

> As professionals, we take pride in our work as the stewards of the nation's infrastructure and value educational and technical advancement. . . . The salary survey results show that our skills are appreciated by the market through compensation and other benefits. Not only is the profession a fun and exciting one, it is also one where you can make a good livelihood.[2]

Civil engineering involves so many different fields that some engineers become specialists while others prefer to be generalists.

Engineers with an interest in ships and the powerful engines that propel them across the water become marine engineers. Others, dedicated to protecting the natural world, might pursue environmental engineering. Specializing in a particular aspect of civil engineering allows individuals to focus their training and careers in the areas in which they are most interested and also allows them to become experts in a particular field. General civil engineers, on the other hand, can take on all sorts of projects, ranging from housing developments to storm-water systems to road-widening projects.

Structural Engineers

One common civil engineering specialty is structural engineering. Structural engineers work with architects to make sure a building's design and the materials planned for its construction will make it strong and stable. If the project is a tall office building, for example, a structural engineer will work out how many beams and columns are needed to make the building sturdy as well as determine the proper thickness of the walls and other important design details. Structural engineers are also involved in road, bridge, pipeline, and tunnel construction projects. Their expertise is especially important on projects that have to stand up to extreme temperatures, high winds, earthquakes, coastal erosion, and other natural forces.

"It's an exciting time to be a civil engineer. As professionals, we take pride in our work as the stewards of the nation's infrastructure."[2]

—Civil engineer Norma Jean Mattei, president of the American Society of Civil Engineers

Structural engineers are also called on to inspect buildings and other projects that are under construction or are recently finished to make sure they are properly constructed. For example, they look at load-bearing walls to make sure they will safely support the roof or other floors above them. They inspect the roof to make sure it is secure. Routine inspections are also crucial for older buildings. Structural engineers check to see how well a building is holding up and look for signs of erosion around a building's foundation or to see if the foundation itself has moved or weakened.

A civil engineer and construction manager discuss progress on a bridge construction project. One of the most diverse engineering fields, civil engineering can involve small projects, such as park drainage, and large projects, such as roads, bridges, pipelines, and tunnels.

Construction Engineers

Construction engineers are another common civil engineering specialty. They design and oversee the construction of roads, bridges, and buildings. Construction engineers have a hand in the many phases of construction. They design the project and estimate its budget, the time needed to complete it, the size and type of construction crew needed for the job, and other aspects of planning and permitting. Construction engineers must take into consideration building materials and any water, sewer, electrical, mechanical, transportation, and environmental concerns. They are on-site for much of a project's construction, working with the project manager to make sure things stay on schedule and to deal with any unexpected problems, such as weather delays or work order changes.

Being a construction engineer means seeing a project through to the final inspection. For Steve Seymour, a construction engineer for OMNNI Associates in Wisconsin, being involved with every stage of a project is especially satisfying. He was the construction engineer on the Fox River Bridge project in Illinois, which went on to win a National Recognition Award from the American Council of Engineering Companies in 2017. The project had unique tasks, such as scheduling construction around the spawning season of a federally protected species of fish. It also had more routine challenges, such as coordinating with state transportation officials to make sure traffic disruptions were kept to a minimum (more than one hundred thousand vehicles cross the bridge daily). "Watching the project progress from the beginning stages of construction to the end is the best part of my job," says Seymour. "I love seeing the transformation take place and know that I was a vital part of it."[3]

Environmental Engineers

Engineers who work on water and wastewater systems and landfills are also civil engineers. Known as environmental engineers, their job is to help protect air, water, and land from becoming polluted by dirty industries, such as oil and gas production, or the processing of chemicals used to make detergents, paint, plastic, and countless other products. "In chemical processing, there's a lot of wastewater to be treated and environmental engineers design systems that monitor them, evaluate performance and modify them for industrial wastewater processes,"[4] says Charles Werth, a professor of environmental engineering at the University of Texas.

Environmental engineers are also brought in to help repair environmental damage caused by pollution or by events such as oil spills. In the massive 2010 Deepwater Horizon oil spill in the Gulf of Mexico, 168 million gallons (636 million L) of oil poured into the gulf over eighty-seven days until the undersea well was capped. Environmental experts worried about the damage this would cause to wildlife, fishing and oyster farming, and local economies that depended on tourism. Environmental engineers tried several solutions to limit the damage. One strategy was to contain parts of the oil floating on the water's surface with inflatable balloons or booms and then burn the oil. Another technique required environmental engineers to work with chemists and marine biologists to release chemicals called dispersants into the oil before it reached

Computer-Aided Design

Whether it is designing a sewer system or a skyscraper, the work of any civil engineer will, at some point, require computer-aided design (CAD). CAD is computer software that civil engineers use to create precise, detailed drawings or technical illustrations. Engineers can create two-dimensional or three-dimensional (3-D) models using CAD. These programs are part of a civil engineer's training and everyday work. A version of CAD, called AutoCAD, is a standard tool used by most civil engineers around the world. In addition to being able to design buildings and other projects on the computer, CAD helps engineers solve geometry and physics equations associated with their designs. Files can be easily saved and sorted. Buildings, water lines, roads, and other parts of a project can be placed in a variety of positions within a job site on the computer. CAD also has a feature that allows an engineer to send a CAD image to a 3-D printer that creates a model of the design. High school students can start learning CAD at school, at home, or at a technical school in their community. Experience with CAD can be a valuable asset when starting an engineering education.

the surface. However, one of the dispersant chemicals used in the Deepwater Horizon cleanup turned out to be harmful to the ecosystem of the gulf. Solving these kinds of problems effectively but safely are among the many important challenges facing environmental engineers.

Materials Engineers

Materials engineers, who are also civil engineers, help develop new materials for use on projects ranging from submarines to spacecraft and from highways to computer chips. They are experts in the properties of metals, ceramics, concrete, wood, fabrics, and other materials used to build things. They must know how various materials will stand up to extreme temperatures, how they will conduct electricity, and whether they will corrode or lose their strength over time.

Rachel Kamish is a materials engineer for a car manufacturer. She specializes in resins, which are chemical compounds used to make plastics. Plastics are a common material used in car manufacturing. Many interior car parts, such as door panels, are made from plastic. Material engineers like Kamish develop plastics that are sturdy, help reduce noise, and are lightweight. Kamish also works on resins that are used for plastics in bumpers and in parts of the engine itself. Kamish describes her work this way: "Be prepared to be a 'jack-of-all-trades.' You have to worry about material properties as well as whether the process to make the resin is going to work. You need to be well-organized and a good people person because you have to interact with a broad range of coworkers."[5]

Transportation Engineers

Transportation engineers are another common type of civil engineer. They work on projects involving the safe and efficient movement of people and goods. They help design highways, railroads, tunnels, bridges, airports, and other transportation projects. The design and construction of large-scale transportation projects are among the most important and most expensive challenges facing transportation engineers. "Unless you have transportation, you don't have much," says transportation engineer Kumares Sinha, who is also a Purdue University engineering professor. "Transportation is the backbone of economies."[6]

To do their job, transportation engineers study traffic patterns and develop solutions to overcrowded highways. They redesign airport runways to make them better able to handle increasingly larger commercial jets and increases in airplane arrivals and departures. Transportation engineers also work with city planners on sidewalks, crosswalks, and bike paths to help people move from one place to another without motorized vehicles. The transportation engineering firm Fehr & Peers, which is based in Washington, DC, works with communities that are dedicated to improving their networks of bicycle paths and lanes. In California's Contra Costa County, for example, Fehr & Peers performed what are known as complete street studies and made recommendations to county officials about bicycle transportation improvements. This complete street concept designs new roads and road improvements to accommodate motorized vehicles, bicycles, and pedestrians. These types of studies are just some of the many types of work performed by transportation engineers.

Marine Engineers

Marine engineers, who are also civil engineers, specialize in designing ships for the US Navy, US Coast Guard, commercial shipping companies, cruise lines, and other entities that put ships to sea. Many marine engineers focus on the internal systems of a ship, such as the steering, heating and cooling, propulsion, and

Geotechnical Engineers Dig Rocks and Soil

One of the less common specialties of civil engineering is geotechnical engineering. Geotechnical engineering focuses on the engineering qualities and behaviors of rocks, minerals, soil, and water. Before a tunnel, bridge, or dam is built, geotechnical engineers determine whether the ground under and around those structures can support them. This is a particularly challenging job when the rock to support a structure is deep underwater. Geotechnical engineers often find jobs with petroleum companies, mining operations, the military, and builders working in areas challenged by earthquakes, landslides, and other natural disasters. These professionals are essential for unusual jobs, such as the storage of hazardous waste in the desert or the construction of oil-drilling facilities in the ocean. Geotechnical engineering is closely aligned with coastal engineering and the construction of piers, oil platforms, marinas, wharves, and beach restoration projects. The work of geotechnical engineers often overlaps with that of geologists and petroleum engineers. Though it is its own discipline within the broader field of civil engineering, geotechnical engineering reaches deeply, so to speak, into many other related industries.

electrical systems. Art Anderson Associates, a marine engineering firm based in Bremerton, Washington, designs and builds boatyards, docks, and other waterfront structures. The firm also refurbishes, designs, and builds a wide range of ships. In 2016 it designed and built the nation's first all-electric ferry to carry cars and people around Puget Sound.

Some marine engineering jobs are less cutting-edge, but they are very important nevertheless. The engineer on an aircraft carrier or an oil tanker, for example, needs to make sure the ship's massive boilers produce enough steam to enable the vessel to reach its destination on time. It is a challenging job, but without a properly functioning engine room, a ship will not get very far. "There are always interesting things that happen aboard ship," says US Navy marine engineer Ron Ingram. "Surprises, things that you wouldn't expect to happen. When a ship is under way in a heavy sea, things come loose that you would never have thought could come loose. Things fail. You've got to get things working again, usually in a hurry."[7]

> "If you enjoy working with people to help solve problems that affect wider society, then go for it. The industry is all about jumping in and trying new solutions."[8]
>
> —Civil engineer Fiona Dixon of the Costain Group

Variety, Challenges, Rewards

The work of a civil engineer is anything but boring and predictable. The workday of one type of civil engineer can be dramatically different from that of another. But no matter where he or she works or in what industry, a civil engineer needs imagination, a little artistic skill, a mind for math, and an openness to working through expected and unexpected challenges. "It's a very rewarding job—there's a great sense of teamwork that comes through creating something and facing challenges together," says Fiona Dixon, an engineer with the Costain Group, a civil engineering firm based in the United Kingdom. "If you enjoy working with people to help solve problems that affect wider society, then go for it. The industry is all about jumping in and trying new solutions."[8]

CHAPTER 2

How Do You Become a Civil Engineer?

Becoming a civil engineer requires a bachelor's degree in civil engineering or one of the specialties or disciplines of civil engineering, such as transportation engineering or materials engineering. To advance in their career, civil engineers usually need to earn a master's degree. A professional engineer (PE) certification is also necessary, as is a license issued by the state where the engineer works. PE certification means an engineer has sufficient training, experience, and knowledge of the rules and responsibilities of the job.

High School Opportunities

Before all that, young people can get a taste of what a civil engineering career is like through high school clubs, internships, job shadowing, and summer camps. Teenagers who want to know more about civil engineering can often find a civil engineer in their community willing to offer some insight into the job. Even shadowing a civil engineer for a day can provide some helpful perspective. Some high schools offer externships, which allow students to spend a few hours a week during their senior year working alongside civil engineers and other professionals.

The ASCE also sponsors high school civil engineering clubs. All that is usually required is a faculty sponsor at the high school, the commitment of a volunteer ASCE member in the community, and a commitment by the school to provide space and support for the club. The ASCE will help interested students and teachers find a local civil engineer to work with the students. The clubs get involved with projects, such as designing and building small bridges and water systems. There are local and national high school competitions for civil engineering clubs too. High school ASCE projects are only small-scale models, but they teach real-world concepts.

A civil engineer shows a group of students one of his projects and explains the types of things he looks for as the project moves forward. Job shadowing is one way for students to learn more about civil engineering.

Civil engineer Jon M. Young is the ASCE's Civil Engineering Club coordinator for the state of Hawaii. He says club activities are not only more interesting than learning engineering from a classroom lecture, book, or video, but they also give students a much better idea of what it means to design and build a project that has a useful purpose. "I think the students are always having fun when they are doing something rather than having to sit and listen to a lecture," says Young. "So anytime you have the students doing an activity like building a marshmallow tower, they enjoy it. I became an engineer because my dad was an engineer, not because I knew anything about it. I think these clubs afford the students a chance to learn about civil engineering."[9]

College

For students entering college with plans to become a civil engineer, a variety of engineering courses await. Other required courses include advanced mathematics (such as calculus and differential equations), mechanics, hydraulics, geotechnics (the study of how the earth's crust interacts with human construction), materials science, and statistics as well as finance and business. Civil engineering students also learn CAD. As students advance in their course work, they design projects, either on their own or as part of a group. A bachelor's degree in engineering usually requires four years of college, but some programs are designed to take five years.

Because civil engineering includes both design and construction elements and touches on so many different disciplines, most university civil engineering programs promote a strong sense of teamwork and collaboration. That is important because a professional civil engineer will work alongside architects, construction supervisors, government representatives, scientists, planners, and many other types of people. "What I appreciate most about the Civil and Environmental Engineering (CEE) program is that it is truly a community," says Massachusetts Institute of Technology CEE major Joshua Hester. "This type of atmosphere fosters a spirit across the many different research areas, as well as friendships and professional relationships after you finish your degree."[10]

Most engineering schools offer some fun hands-on learning opportunities too. The Student Steel Bridge Competition is a popular activity that draws civil engineering student teams from universities across the country. The competition calls upon students to design, fabricate (shape and bend the parts), and construct a steel bridge that can hold 2,500 pounds (1,134 kg) and is 23 feet (7 m) long and 3 feet (0.9 m) high. "I'm in Steel Bridge just to get to connect with more of my classmates, and to share a mutual love of bridges with each other," says Iowa State University civil engineering major Kara Kieffer. "I worked a job that I got to help design and inspect bridges, and that's kind of where I really fell in love with it."[11]

> "I worked a job that I got to help design and inspect bridges, and that's kind of where I really fell in love with it."[11]
>
> —Iowa State University civil engineering major Kara Kieffer

Internships: Necessary Training

Civil engineering internships are crucial to getting on-the-job training as well as for making an impression on possible future

Civilian Engineering in the Military

Even though the word *civil* in *civil engineering* stands for "civilian" and was first used to distinguish it from military engineering, that distinction no longer applies. Every branch of the armed forces has a civil engineering corps or division. These military civil engineers help design and build facilities such as airports and runways, docks, and other structures—often in inhospitable places and battlefield conditions around the world. The most well-known military civil engineering organization is the US Army Corps of Engineers, which oversees the dredging of waterways and the building and maintaining of military facilities within the United States and abroad.

It is not uncommon for students to attend engineering school and join the military. As part of this arrangement, the military covers the cost of a college education, but upon graduation the student owes the military five years of service. Some people spend their whole career in the military. The experience gained in the military also prepares a person for a civilian civil engineering career. Even if a young person enters the military with an engineering education and work experience in the field, he or she must attend a program such as the Naval Civil Engineer Corps Officers School to get training in the specific civil engineering needs of the military.

employers. Rebecca Clark, a civil engineer and project manager with the large construction company Skansa USA, recommends students participate in as many co-ops and work-related chances as possible in college. The term *co-op* stands for cooperative education. Co-ops combine classroom education and on-the-job training for students. "Co-ops are great," she says. "When I was in college I always had internships and I think, to me, those were priceless. A lot of people we hire end up coming through our co-op or internship programs. It gives the student and the company a chance to assess fit."[12]

The Georgia Institute of Technology (Georgia Tech), for example, offers an undergraduate co-op program that provides engineering students with three semesters of paid work experience away from campus. It means taking five years to get a civil engineering degree instead of four, but the co-op program gives students substantial work experience even before they get their diplomas.

Other schools also encourage students to get their internship experience in while they are still enrolled. At the Florida Institute of Technology (Florida Tech), juniors or seniors complete an internship with a local civil engineering firm. In a similar vein, Florida Tech and other engineering schools require seniors to complete a capstone project before graduating. A capstone project is meant to simulate real-world situations. It requires several presentations of a student's work to professors and professional engineers. Past capstone projects at Florida Tech have included a completely submersible remote-controlled airplane and a camera system for a parking lot that identifies empty spaces and makes their locations known to motorists trying to find a parking space.

Civil engineering students get practical experience designing and building the kinds of projects they will work on when they are professionals. But these programs offer much more than hands-on experience. Student efforts can be inspiring, reminders of why they wanted to pursue this field in the first place. "Being able to tangibly visualize the real-world application of the knowledge I have acquired in my classes in these projects allowed me to see my coursework in a refreshing and practical light," Cornell University civil engineering major Morgan Mills says of her internship. "It also inspired and challenged me to think more deeply about inventive ways to implement what I have learned."[13]

"Being able to tangibly visualize the real-world application of the knowledge I have acquired in my classes in these projects allowed me to see my coursework in a refreshing and practical light."[13]

—Cornell University civil engineering major Morgan Mills

Starting a Career

Once students have obtained their engineering degree, they still have more studying and testing ahead. Civil engineers need to pass the Fundamentals of Engineering (FE) exam, a 110-question test that takes six hours. The civil engineering FE exam includes many math and science questions, but it is mostly concerned with the test taker's knowledge of materials, fluid mechanics, structural analysis, structural design, transportation engineering, and other subjects related to their particular specialty. After passing the FE, an engineer is able to work on a limited basis.

Obtaining a PE license is necessary to obtain government contracts and perform other work in the field. Earning that license requires four years of work under a licensed PE and passage of the PE exam. Each PE exam is designed for a specific engineering discipline, such as civil engineering. However, chemical engineers, electrical engineers, and other kinds of engineers must also pass PE exams specific to their fields. It is usually an eight-hour, eighty-question test, though the structural engineering PE exam is sixteen hours, taken over two days. Some states may have additional requirements to obtain a professional civil engineering license. Likewise, throughout their careers civil engineers are required to take part in ongoing training and class work to maintain their licenses.

For new civil engineers who have decided on a discipline, the aim should be to find a firm that is looking for entry-level professionals in that field. For example, a civil engineer who wants to specialize in transportation should apply at firms that specialize in transportation. Those who are unsure about a particular direction should seek out a job with a multidisciplinary civil engineering firm. That type of company will likely have civil engineers who can do site planning, water and sewer design, road and building design, construction services, permitting, inspections, and other aspects of civil engineering. That way, they can gain experience in a variety of disciplines and either develop one area of interest or continue as a generalist.

CHAPTER 3

What Skills and Personal Qualities Matter Most— and Why?

Strong math and science (especially physics) skills are very important for success as a civil engineer. For example, designing highway curves that allow for safe high-speed travel is one civil engineering challenge—and it requires a solid knowledge of geometry and physics. The same is true for a municipal water system that carries drinking water from a treatment plant to thousands of homes and businesses. "Engineering is all about equations, math relations, calculations and numbers,"[14] says civil engineer Deborah Suazo-Davila of the US Army Corps of Engineers.

There are, however, plenty of other skills and qualities that are common among most successful civil engineers. It is not enough to be a good math student. Engineers have to be able to work with others and build relationships. Atlanta-based civil engineer Emmy Montanye explained this to an audience of civil engineering students at her alma mater, Georgia Tech. "I can guarantee you that no one is this room will be successful as a one-person act," she said. "Nobody in this room is going to be a leader if they have no one to lead."[15]

Confident, Curious, Clever

Success as a civil engineer starts with a genuine interest in how things work and a desire to solve problems. Of course, being able to come up with solutions and presenting them confidently is really what the job is all about. Engineers are born problem solvers. They like to size up a challenge and come up with an answer.

A civil engineer who is overseeing relocation of a bicycle path during a road expansion project might have to obtain permits, conduct traffic studies, and address concerns of local residents at public meetings.

With civil engineering, the challenges are often very big: How to get large groups of people from one place to another safely and efficiently? How to protect a city from rising flood waters? How to transport the materials necessary to build a colony on Mars?

But civil engineering also means solving smaller problems, like improving the drainage in an older neighborhood or relocating a bicycle path during a road expansion project. A civil engineer who is working on a project of this type might have to address government or resident concerns about pollution or construction noise and road blockages. The engineer will also be responsible for various other tasks, including obtaining permits, overseeing work crews, doing traffic studies, and taking soil samples. Overcoming these seemingly ordinary challenges helps people enjoy their communities more and keeps them and their homes safe. They are among the rewards enjoyed by civil engineers.

Civil engineers, like other types of engineers, are also curious about the world around them. Seeing beachfront erosion, a civil engineer might wonder how and why that happens and how it can be stopped. Or seeing a high-speed train traveling down a track, a civil engineer might think about how that train can be made to go even faster without sacrificing safety. There is so much in the world to be curious about, says Laura Marino, who graduated with a civil engineering degree from Stanford University. "I knew that I was going to go into engineering, because I liked science," she says. "I was always curious about how things work, why things work."[16]

Creative Designers

Many civil engineers are artists at heart. The opportunities to help design modern buildings and cities and to offer creative solutions to real-world challenges are often what draw people to civil engineering. It is not uncommon for an art student with strong math skills to consider civil engineering as a way to combine both skills and interests. "I really enjoy using math and applying it to real world situations as well as using my creative side and designing things,"[17] says Lilian Garcia, a civil engineering major at the University of Colorado.

> "I really enjoy using math and applying it to real world situations as well as using my creative side and designing things."[17]
>
> —Lilian Garcia, a civil engineering major at the University of Colorado

Civil engineering is more than designing something cool and useful. It is also about imagining solutions or improvements that no one has thought of before. "I want to be a very flexible construction engineer who's able to tackle any project thrown at me and think of solutions from a creative perspective," says Sadie Argus, a construction engineering and management student researching the challenges of Mars exploration at Purdue University. "That's always been my goal. I love outside-the-box projects and thinking about new ways to construct something. So, this research has definitely helped me learn to be flexible and push my boundaries as an engineer."[18]

Jacks-of-All-Trades

Civil engineers must understand many areas of design and construction, especially early in their career, before they decide whether to specialize. If there is a problem with drainage on a project, a civil engineer will need to come up with a way to prevent standing water from delaying the project. If the electrical system for a tunnel's lights needs to be expanded in the middle of construction, the civil engineer on the project needs to have ideas to boost the system while the wiring and lights are still accessible.

> "I love outside-the-box projects and thinking about new ways to construct something."[18]
>
> —Sadie Argus, a construction engineering and management major at Purdue University

Although many civil engineers choose to specialize in a particular discipline, others make a good living working on a variety of engineering projects. Even those who do specialize need to have some expertise in structural engineering, land use, hydraulics, electronics, permitting, and business. A willingness to learn about a wide variety of subjects is a vital skill for civil engineers, especially early in their careers. Muhyadin Artan, a civil engineering graduate of Ohio State University, says "My first piece of advice to a prospective civil engineer is to avoid limiting yourself to one area of civil engineering, such as transportation, structural, etc., as you will likely be involved in projects that contain more than one sub discipline of civil engineering."[19]

Professionalism

The way a civil engineer works, both alone and when collaborating with others, will determine how far he or she can go in this profession. Civil engineers must be detail oriented and possess good communication, organization, and multitasking skills.

Although being able to see the big picture is essential, civil engineers must also pay great attention to detail. They must think of all the things that could go wrong and design and build their projects to avoid those troubles. If a building collapses or a road system leads to accidents or unsafe travel, the civil engineer is one of the people responsible for that failure.

And from a business standpoint, making sure that the wording is right in a contract can mean the difference between making or losing money on the job. "To have an eye for detail is crucial," says

Syn Dee Chua, another Ohio State University civil engineering grad. "Construction plans and contract documents have a lot of fine print and we have to make sure that everything is accounted for in a bid, or risk not being awarded [the] project."[20]

Communication skills are also critical. Civil engineers must work with many people on a project, so it is important that they can explain what is needed at every stage of the process. And because civil engineers have to work with clients, citizens, permitting authorities, and many other groups, the need for effective communication skills cannot be overstated. "Being able to communicate clearly and professionally is also another valuable skill,"

Retaining Engineering Students Through Art

It is not unusual for a student to arrive on a college campus excited about majoring in civil engineering only to be turned off by dry engineering courses. These students chose civil engineering because they dreamed of designing beautiful bridges and airports of the future. Instead, the artistic side of engineering seems lost amid the lessons about hydraulics and materials science. As a result, civil engineering and many other science, technology, engineering, and math (STEM) majors choose another path.

To help combat this STEM drain, the National Science Foundation teamed up with civil engineering professors and researchers at several universities on the Advancing the Dissemination of the Creative Art of Structural/Civil Engineering project. The main goal is to transform introductory civil engineering courses by emphasizing the artistic and design aspects of the subject. Researchers at schools such as Princeton University and the University of Massachusetts, Amherst, are hoping that this might draw students who were not on a STEM track into civil engineering. By changing the perception of civil engineers as creative artists rather than just technicians, universities may help retain talented civil engineering students and attract those who pictured themselves as artists first and foremost.

Chua says. "There will always be questions and things that need clarification, and the most effective way to solve a problem is to be able to communicate and converse clearly—whether it is in-person, through a phone call, or an email. As engineers, or 'technical people,' being able to communicate a technical problem to non-technical people is a key skill."[21]

The most successful civil engineers also learn how to multi-task. A civil engineer may have several projects going at once, all at various stages of development. While one project may be early in the design phase, another may be nearing completion. It is essential that a civil engineer not only be able to keep multiple projects organized when they are at various stages but also that he or she be nimble enough to react to changing conditions on a project or shifting demands from a client or government agency. "I am coordinating complex, evolving projects and must keep a large number of stakeholders informed and updated," says construction engineer and project manager Andrew Salt. "Just as important are organizational skills. I work on multiple projects at a time, all in different stages of development. Flexibility is also key. I often have to adapt to project challenges as they arise, and adjust accordingly."[22]

CHAPTER 4

What Is It Like to Work as a Civil Engineer?

The closet of a civil engineer is often a study in contrasts. Whereas one side of the closet might contain expensive dress clothes and shoes, the other side might hold jeans and work boots with a little touch of stubborn dirt around the edges. That is because a civil engineer can spend part of the day working in an air-conditioned office, sitting at a computer and working with state-of-the-art design software, and another part of the day out in the field. For some marine engineers, the job can take them from an office one day to the middle of the ocean the next day, checking to see how their ship design or their boiler design is functioning out on the waves. And if permanent structures are ever built on the moon or on Mars, civil engineers will likely be in pressurized space suits overseeing all the details.

What Is in a Workday?

A civil engineer's day can include some combination of designing at a desk, meeting with clients and collaborators, overseeing construction on a job site, doing research for a current or possible future project, making phone calls, and solving dilemmas big and small. "There's no such thing as a typical day," says civil engineer Fiona Dixon.

> My role basically involves translating designs on to the construction site, so my time is split between the office and the site, where I supervise and check the construction activities. Every project is different: I currently work a 50-hour, five-day week. In a year's time I could be working nights in another part of the country. But there are options to suit everyone.[23]

Patricia Frayre, a civil engineer with the firm Walter P. Moore in Texas, says big projects demand an engineer's attention to countless issues. Frayre was one of the main designers of the new Harris County Convention Center in Houston, which required extensive research on existing utilities, transportation concerns, and the other needs and functions of the massive downtown complex. "You have to co-ordinate with the different agencies that will be reviewing the designs and issuing permits and make sure that everything works," she says. "Parking lots have to drain. Pipes have to be sized accordingly. Most importantly, coordination with the other disciplines like the MEPs (mechanical, electrical and plumbing engineers), structural engineers, and, of course, the architects has to occur."[24]

> "There's no such thing as a typical day."[23]
>
> —Civil engineer Fiona Dixon

Where the Jobs Are

Civil engineers work in every state in the United States and in every nation around the world. Wherever roads, bridges, water and sewer systems, ships, marinas, new buildings, and other large-scale structures are being built, civil engineers are hard at work.

They can work in the private sector or for the government. A private-sector civil engineer can be self-employed or work for a company that has two civil engineers or two hundred. There are civil engineering firms that have branches in several countries and work on major international projects. There are civil engineers right now designing and constructing housing, transportation, and other projects that will not be finished for years to come. "Our day-to-day lives depend on the infrastructure around us that is designed, built and maintained by civil engineers—from roads, railways and bridges to energy, water and waste networks," says Richard Coackley, former president of the Institution of Civil Engineers. "It forms the backbone of society and the economy."[25]

From Design to Construction

Regardless of the size of the project, civil engineering is still a matter of designing and building something useful. It may be a structure, such as a tunnel or an oil refinery, or it may be a pond to collect storm water runoff. But in the end, it is about providing society with something new or something improved that will be used by a lot of people for a long time. A civil engineer's work often begins months or years before any construction or renovation starts.

Before a single mound of dirt is moved on a project, a civil engineer must conduct feasibility studies to see whether the project can be done as envisioned at the site, investigate the property where the work will be done, design the project, obtain permits, and work with all other interested parties on the planning of the project. For example, a civil engineer could be hired by a city to design a new park that will include a soccer field, playground, picnic area, and parking lot. The civil engineer must then survey the future park site and start to figure out how best to fit those features onto the property. On a project of this type, a civil engineer might consider questions like these:

"Our day-to-day lives depend on the infrastructure around us that is designed, built and maintained by civil engineers."[25]

—Richard Coackley, former president of the Institution of Civil Engineers

- Does the elevation on all or part of the property need to be raised or lowered?
- How will vehicles enter and exit the park?
- How will pedestrians reach the park?
- How many parking spaces will be needed, and how should they be arranged?
- What is the best drainage plan to make sure the soccer field, playground, picnic area, and parking lot do not flood in rainy weather?
- What materials will be needed for the parking lot and playground?

Those are just some of the questions to be answered before design work begins. An engineer will usually have deadlines to submit preliminary plans to the people overseeing the project. If those plans are approved, more detailed design work is done until the final plans are approved. After that the civil engineer will work

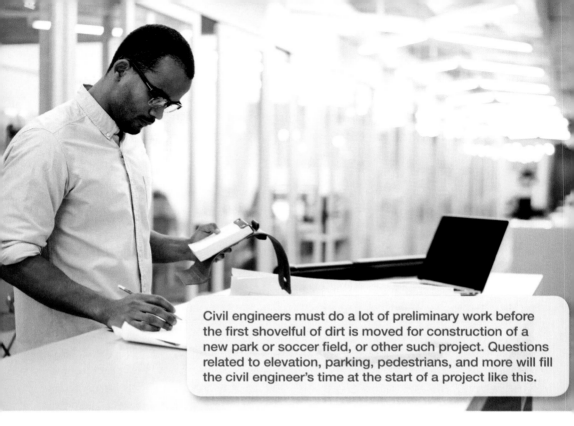

Civil engineers must do a lot of preliminary work before the first shovelful of dirt is moved for construction of a new park or soccer field, or other such project. Questions related to elevation, parking, pedestrians, and more will fill the civil engineer's time at the start of a project like this.

with the project manager to hire the various contractors to get the property ready, install utility lines, build the entrance and exit roads to the property, create the parking spaces, and handle any other work that is needed to complete the park.

The civil engineer will also work with other parties involved in the project's construction. A civil engineer is often the main liaison between the company doing the work and those responsible for the project, such as the owner of the property or the government agency that will be responsible for maintaining the project. The engineer helps make sure that the various crews on a job have the materials they need when they need them and that any changes in plans or deadlines are coordinated with all the parties involved.

The engineer needs to be available to solve any problems that come up. In the case of the park, for example, city officials might decide that the lighting for the park needs to be changed due to concern from neighbors. The civil engineer on the project would help come up with a solution to keep the project on sched-ule and satisfy the city and nearby residents. In some cases, midconstruction problems are related to health or environmental concerns. Civil engineer Avi Estrin was monitoring the construction of a large housing development in New Zealand when work crews discovered old underground pipes coated with asbestos. The asbestos had contaminated much of the soil around the pipes. Estrin had to coordinate the closing of the construction site, adjust the construction schedule, and arrange for specialists to come in, remove the pipes, and decontaminate the area.

Once a project is completed, a civil engineer may play a role in maintaining it for a specified time. Eventually, the park (or building or airport, etc.) will be the responsibility of the government or property owner that commissioned the project. But for an initial period spelled out in the contract, the project manager and civil

When a Civil Engineer Goes to Sea

Most civil engineering work is on land. But one type of civil engineer, the marine engineer, often works aboard ships in the middle of the ocean. This work often involves keeping a ship's engine humming and the rest of the vessel's functions running smoothly too. Marine engineers might work on a ship's big turbine engines, its air-conditioning systems, its propellers, and other equipment. And often this is done on choppy seas hundreds or thousands of miles from parts suppliers and manufacturers.

Resourcefulness is especially important for marine engineers. Being a marine engineer can be challenging, but it is not without its unique rewards, explains Canadian marine engineer Martin Leduc. "Basically, we must be knowledgeable enough to recognize a problem, then either fix it, make due, or call in the specialists," he says. "We deal with it. Out in the middle of the Atlantic, there's not many auto parts stores, and even less room for excuses."

Martin Leduc, "An Interview with a Marine Engineer," Martin's Marine Engineering Page, 2015. www.diesel duck.info.

engineer (sometimes the same person) will make sure all the bugs are worked out. If problems arise during this time, the civil engineer will have to come up with solutions.

Once the design and construction part of the job ends, a civil engineering project takes on a new life. It becomes a useful part of a community, enjoyed by people long into the future. It is a lasting example of a civil engineer's hard work. "The most fun thing about my job is seeing something you've designed being constructed or people using the facilities after construction," Frayre says. "Seeing a clear site or something on site that gets torn down and replaced with new construction is a very satisfying part of this job."[26]

Advancement and Other Job Opportunities

Some civil engineers are content to spend their careers designing and building whatever projects land on their desks. But others want to move into supervisory roles, such as project manager or chief engineer, or into an executive position like the chief operating officer of a large civil engineering firm. Advancement means more responsibility—and usually more money. Moving up may also allow an engineer to have more say in what projects he or she works on.

Civil engineers usually start their careers by working for a private company or a local government. They are often assigned smaller, less technically demanding parts of a project until they gain more experience. Entry-level work might include drafting construction or bid documents, analyzing data from environmental studies, taking soil samples, and doing a wide variety of other tasks.

Getting an Advanced Degree

An advanced degree, such as a master's in civil engineering, construction or industrial management, or another specialty, is usually required to move up the ranks to project manager and beyond. Becoming a top-level manager almost always means having more than a bachelor's degree. Certainly, earning a master of business administration (MBA) would benefit an engineer with a particular interest in the business side of consulting. "For me, the decision to pursue an MBA stemmed from a desire to tackle larger and more abstract strategic problems instead of the structured 'engineering type' problems I was accustomed to," says Charlie Briston, an MBA student at Georgia Tech. "The strong analytical capability that engineers possess is highly valued in the business world, but it is imperative that you also understand the other, more qualitative, aspects. These qualitative skills are what engineers stereotypically lack; we like black and white answers, but in the business world, it's not typically that simple,"[27] he notes.

Advancement also demands years of experience—there are no shortcuts. But there are some things to consider when it comes to planning a long, successful career in civil engineering. The ASCE suggests forming a long-term vision that includes work, family, and lifestyle, and then reviewing it periodically. Having a short-term plan that is updated frequently is also recommended. A mentor who will provide career and life guidance can be very helpful. A mentor could be a college professor or an older engineer willing to offer advice and insight. Also beneficial is a willingness to change career directions and consider possibilities that were not in the short- or long-term plans.

> "Work hard for what you want in lieu of feeling you are entitled to what you want."[28]
>
> —Amanda Schimmoeller, a civil engineer with the Turner Construction Company

Amanda Schimmoeller, a civil engineer with the Turner Construction Company in Columbus, Ohio, offers three additional pieces of advice to new engineers hoping to advance their careers. "First, gather as much exposure to hands-on applications and experiences, so you can have a better understanding of what you are managing and designing," she says. "Second, network; this is a key strategy in any industry you choose to pursue. Lastly, work hard for what you want in lieu of feeling you are entitled to what you want."[28]

Once a civil engineering career begins, the nature of other job opportunities and advancement will depend on the ambitions of the engineer, the job market, and the career path the engineer chooses. Working in the private sector can mean working at a large or small firm, working independently, or working as an in-house engineer for a petroleum company, construction company, or other business that requires civil engineers. Government employment can range from small towns to the federal government, including the military.

Researching the Possibilities

Civil engineers interested in the long-term future of their industry or in simply discovering the next useful innovation to help people live and work better or safer, may find research a rewarding career path. Researchers at universities, as well as at government and corporate facilities, are developing better highway materials; more efficient pollution controls; hydraulic, wind, and solar energy systems; and many other innovations. At the University of Buffalo's Department of Civil, Structural, and Environmental Engineering, students and educators are researching new materials that can make large bridge supports sturdier and less vulnerable to wind and waves.

While a civil engineering student at the University at Buffalo (UB) in 2014, Deshawn Henry developed a solar water heater that kills 99 percent of bacteria and pathogens in the water. His hope is that this kind of simple but vital technology can help people in developing nations who have limited access to clean, drinkable water. "I have seen how intense research activities can inspire UB students and educate the next generation of innovators," says James Jensen, an engineering professor at the university. "Deshawn's work would allow a family in sunny regions to treat drinking water without having to expend energy or rely on imported technologies."

Marcene Robinson, "Student's Six-Foot Water and Solar-Powered Lens Purifies Polluted Water," University at Buffalo, School of Engineering and Applied Sciences, August 14, 2014. http://engineering.buffalo.edu.

The Private Sector

Many civil engineers start out working for firms that are hired by governments for specific projects such as a new road, water treatment plant, airport, or marina. These are often design projects, though a consultant may be hired for both design and construction. A smaller firm means working on numerous and varied projects. This gives beginning engineers exposure to a wide range of projects. An engineer may then choose to specialize in a particular type of work. That engineer can then try to become an expert in that field and form his or her own firm or move on to a larger firm that specializes in that work. Engineers who like a variety of projects may also form their own companies that offer a range of services. Working for a larger firm can mean focusing attention on fewer, but bigger, projects. Bigger companies offer more opportunities for advancement, but moving around may be necessary if a firm has offices in many locations.

One of the great payoffs of working at a large firm is the opportunity to work on a variety of projects in a variety of places. This was the case for Caro-Joy Barendse, a South African civil engineer who specializes in airport work. She worked her way up from an entry-level engineer to a project manager for an international engineering firm based in the Netherlands. "I now have exposure to not only engineering design projects, but also business strategy and airport planning projects," Barendse says. "I also get to work on an international scale, on projects based in different countries, and work with people from various countries and cultures, so my job is always interesting and challenging."[29]

Public Sector

In addition to working directly on government-sponsored infrastructure projects, government civil engineers can move into areas where they help develop policy and standards for the industry. Engineers with these goals are advised to get additional training in public administration and business management. Because government civil engineers interact with citizens, communication skills and patience are particularly valuable. "As a public servant, there are occasions that require me to contact a constituent/resident, and the ability to convey my message to them in a non-technical way is a very important skill,"[30] says Muhyadin Artan, a civil engineer with the city of Columbus, Ohio.

Government civil engineers often work with local or state planners on land-use decisions and projects such as new school construction, highway

"As a public servant, there are occasions that require me to contact a constituent/resident, and the ability to convey my message to them in a non-technical way is a very important skill."[30]

—Muhyadin Artan, a civil engineer with the city of Columbus, Ohio extensions, water and sewer utility expansions, airport improvements, and other infrastructure projects. Depending on the project, a government may have to hire an engineering or construction contractor to do the work. A civil engineer working for a city or county, for example, may act as a liaison between government officials and the contractors. A government engineer may also become a public works director, overseeing the roads and utilities departments.

The Path to Project Manager

Every civil engineering project needs a manager—whether it is a multi-million-dollar endeavor that takes years to complete or a smaller job that is done in a few months. A project manager is responsible for all aspects of a project, including its planning, execution, and closing. Project managers define projects, establish schedules, manage budgets, assemble teams to carry out the work, oversee employees and contractors, and much more. Because project management can mean more money, more responsibility, and more interest from employers, a growing number of civil engineers are earning the project management professional (PMP) certification and are honing their management skills. A PMP certification recognizes that an engineer has taken courses and has acquired the work experience to be an effective project manager.

Civil engineer Anthony Fasano, the author of *Engineering Your Success*, says one of most helpful steps on the way to becoming a project manager is to hold off deciding on a specific discipline of civil engineering. His early work experience included structural design for bridges, hydraulic modeling for home and commercial sites, and land surveying. "While civil engineering is broad, many of the different disciplines are interrelated," he says. "So having knowledge in the different areas has been instrumental to my success as a project manager."

Anthony Fasano, "The Best Advice Anyone Ever Gave Me as a Young Engineer," Engineering.com, April 24, 2013. www.engineering.com.

Educating Future Engineers

Some civil engineers opt to move away from the design and construction parts of their field altogether. Instead, they choose to teach what they have learned or move into research. Teaching the next generation of civil engineers is an option for those who prefer to work in a university setting. In addition to earning a PE license, an engineer should have several years of real-world experience before pursuing an academic career. A doctorate in civil engineering is required before becoming a college professor. Earning a PhD can take two to four years, depending on the program and whether an engineer attends school full-time or part-time.

In order to advance as a civil engineering professor, it is often necessary to take whatever teaching opportunities are available and to get published. Writing papers that appear in civil engineering professional or academic journals, and writing books, gives a professor a higher profile and helps with career advancement. In addition to teaching, civil engineers in academia also are consulted to help establish new industry standards for various disciplines.

Civil engineering professors are often consulted as experts in specific disciplines. For example, Dario Gasparini, a civil engineering professor at Case Western Reserve University, is a world-renowned expert on historic bridges and structural engineering. He assisted the town of Gorham, New Hampshire, in preserving and refurbishing a beautiful wooden bridge from the mid-nineteenth century that was damaged by an arsonist in 2004. The bridge's trusses were repaired at Case Western in Ohio before being shipped back to New England to be placed in their original location. "It's a really nice story; it is nice that this bridge was salvaged," Gasparini says. "It came from Gorham and now it's going back at Gorham."[31]

Those who pursue careers in civil engineering will likely not be disappointed. This field offers many possibilities. Whether they work in the private or public sector, whether they are involved in the design and construction of projects or in teaching up-and-coming engineers, civil engineers will encounter an ever-changing and always interesting career.

CHAPTER 6

What Does the Future Hold for Civil Engineers?

As long as people need places to live, work, and play, civil engineers will be in demand. In the United States, the demand will be especially great in the years ahead. That is because many of the nation's roads, tunnels, rail lines, inland waterways, drinking water systems, dams, airports, and other infrastructure are aging and badly need upgrades or replacements. The ASCE issues a so-called infrastructure report card for the country every four years. In 2017 the overall grade was a D+. Some categories received decent grades (rail infrastructure received a B, for example), but others were not given very good marks. Public transit systems (not including railroads) were given a D-, and aviation, dams, drinking water, and roads all received a D grade. Bridges, ports, and solid waste each received a C+. The letter grades refer to the physical health of the infrastructure, any safety risks it poses, how efficiently it handles its current demand, its capacity to handle future growth, and other criteria.

ASCE leaders say improving the country's infrastructure will require the vision and skills of the next generation of civil engineers as well as a commitment by elected leaders to invest money in projects large and small. "While our nation's infrastructure problems are significant, they are solvable," says ASCE president Norma Jean Mattei. "We need our elected leaders— those who pledged to rebuild our infrastructure while on the campaign trail—to follow through on those promises with investment

> "While our nation's infrastructure problems are significant, they are solvable."[32]
>
> —Norma Jean Mattei, president of the American Society of Civil Engineers

and innovative solutions that will ensure our infrastructure is built for the future."[32] About twenty thousand civil engineering jobs are expected to open up yearly for the next decade or so. Transportation engineers in particular will be in demand as major highway improvement projects are a high priority of the federal government.

New Fields of Exploration

The future will also present some exciting challenges and opportunities for civil engineers in areas such as energy production, space exploration, and transportation. Renewable energy production is growing globally, but making solar and wind power economically viable remains a challenge. Plans to return to the moon, explore Mars, and make space travel available to the public are driving the demand for civil, mechanical, and electrical engineers with an interest in the cosmos. Here on Earth, transportation engineers are addressing the challenges involved with driverless vehicles on land and water as well as drones in the airspace around airports and urban areas.

The move away from fossil fuels will require power grids that rely on solar, wind, and hydroelectric energy. Civil engineers who can design and build such systems will be valuable in all parts of the world. David Evans, the chairman and founder of the civil engineering firm David Evans and Associates in Portland, Oregon, says that civil engineers in the years ahead will be needed not only for the design of large-scale solar, wind, and other energy projects but also for all the infrastructure needed to support these renewable energy systems. "There clearly is a big opportunity for civil engineering firms to provide services to the power and energy market," Evans says. "Energy clients need civil engineering firms to prepare permit applications; design roads, sites, foundations, and storm water control systems; and to conduct geotechnical investigations. Wind systems, in particular, require heavy civil design to provide construction and maintenance access to and foundations for each of the turbines."[33]

Civil engineers are not bound by the environments and physical laws of Earth, however. Establishing research facilities, mining operations, and colonies on the moon, Mars, and elsewhere in

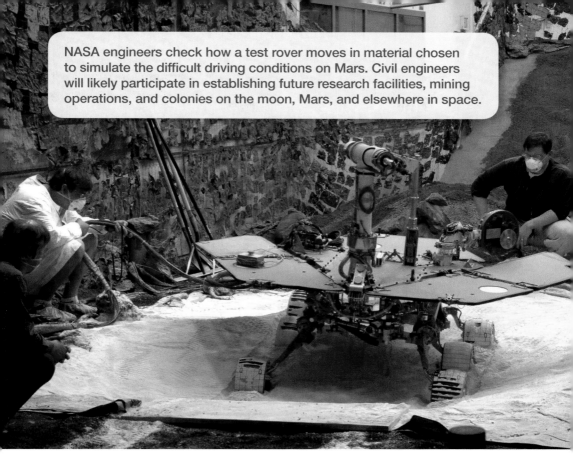

NASA engineers check how a test rover moves in material chosen to simulate the difficult driving conditions on Mars. Civil engineers will likely participate in establishing future research facilities, mining operations, and colonies on the moon, Mars, and elsewhere in space.

space will need civil engineers leading the way. "Civil and construction engineering expertise are crucial if humans are to go to Mars and settle," says Sarag Saikia, a professor who teaches the civil engineering course called the Human Journey to Mars at Purdue University. "They will be crucial in preparing the landing site, base, and plan to find and extract valuable in situ [local] resources such as water or other minerals. The civil and construction engineers will identify capabilities and resources that will be key to establishing a sustainable human presence on Mars."[34]

Back on Earth, civil engineers in the transportation industry envision a future of driverless electric cars, more high-speed trains, and faster, safer air travel. For example, billions of federal dollars have been earmarked for a major expansion of high-speed rail in the United States under the American Recovery and Reinvestment Act. "There will be expanded opportunities for civil engineering students as a result of this initiative in the United

States,"[35] says Christopher Barkan, a professor and the director of the railroad engineering program at the University of Illinois at Urbana-Champaign.

Next-Gen Technology

Like most other engineering fields, civil engineering is constantly changing with the times. For example, as new sources of energy or new building materials become available, civil engineers must be able to adapt their designs and construction to accommodate these new technologies. Materials engineers will be needed to create more efficient and less-expensive construction materials to improve energy efficiency and allow for massive infrastructure improvements in places such as Africa. As more antipollution or safety requirements are placed on buildings and utility systems,

A Career with a Strong Future

Even with advances in artificial intelligence, robotics, and other technologies, certain professions, such as doctors and teachers, will always be needed. The same can be said of civil engineers. They are needed at all times, regardless of how the economy is doing or what news is in the headlines. In economically robust times, civil engineers are needed to design and build new structures to accommodate more spending and growth. When a recession hits and new construction halts, civil engineers are called on to help repair the old infrastructure and give it new life. And if the space program boldly goes forward with plans to further explore Mars and the moon, the opportunities for civil engineers could really take off.

While there are no guarantees about job security and job growth, civil engineering has a built-in advantage over other disciplines. People will never stop needing places to work and live, and they will never stop needing the means to travel back and forth to those places. For young people with a talent for math and a desire to make a contribution to society, there is no end in sight for a career in civil engineering.

civil engineers must be ready to work within new laws and regulations. This can be challenging but also exciting. Civil engineers are building the future environments where people will live, work, travel, and play.

The next generation of civil engineers also will have to be more learned in digital technology and be able to comfortably work across the boundaries of other engineering disciplines, such as mechanical and electrical engineering. "A road now includes sensors and communications equipment; it's not just a bit of blacktop," says Sharon Kindleysides, the managing director of Kapsch TrafficCom, a global company specializing in intelligent transportation systems, adding,

> There is a blurring of boundaries, and you can't cubbyhole things any more. You've got roads talking to vehicles, and traffic lights talking to cars. When we start looking at autonomous vehicles, we will have to have changes in the rulebook, and we have got to stop having these divisions between civil engineering, mechanical engineering, architecture, etc.[36]

Future Growth

The civil engineering field is expected to grow about 11 percent per year through 2026. That is better than many technical fields, and if state and federal governments truly commit to ambitious infrastructure improvements, that growth rate could jump much higher.

Also fueling that growth are global modernization efforts. Parts of the world that have never had modern highways, dams, bridges, and networks to provide power and water are welcoming civil engineers and their crews to help them modernize. These areas include rural parts of North America, huge swaths of Africa, and other regions across the globe. A rising global population, with more people moving to cities, will require more civil engineers with expertise in pollution control, clean water systems, transportation, and safe waste disposal. Rising sea levels may also increase the demand for engineers to help manage coastal erosion

> "Civil engineers are often unsung heroes, working behind the scenes to make society better and safer."[37]
>
> —Robert Mair, current president of the Institution of Civil Engineers

problems and to adapt coastal communities to deal with encroaching seas.

Whether it is enjoying a clean glass of water from the kitchen faucet or zooming across a mighty river-spanning bridge, people rely on the work of civil engineers just about everywhere. And that is not likely to change anytime soon. "Civil engineers are often unsung heroes, working behind the scenes to make society better and safer," says Robert Mair, the president of the Institution of Civil Engineers. "We often take for granted the benefits of modern life—from our energy supplies to sanitation to our ability to travel—and many people are unaware that civil engineering makes these things possible."[37]

CHAPTER 7

Interview with a Civil Engineer

Erica Floyd is a civil engineer with Gulf Civil Engineering in Pensacola, Florida. She founded the company in 2012 after working for other civil engineering firms in the region. Floyd discussed her career with the author via e-mail.

Q: Why did you become a civil engineer?

A: I was a good student all throughout middle and high school. I enjoyed math and always had an interest in art. It took some time to find my way after graduation, but eventually I went to a technical school for computer-aided drafting. It seemed to be a nice combination of . . . math and art. Eventually I got a job as a drafter for an engineering firm. After a year of working for a professional engineer, my employer recommended that I return to school to study engineering. I took his advice and graduated cum laude with a BS in civil engineering from the University of South Alabama.

Q: Can you describe your typical workday?

A: A typical workday could consist of a day in the office designing the site infrastructure for a hospital, subdivision, or commercial retail facility. The infrastructure could include roadways, parking lots, water and sewer services, or storm water systems. Days are also spent on site, inspecting the construction of a project we have designed. Sometimes, I spend time in meetings with clients, contractors, and/or local regulatory agencies discussing the future of a project. In the case of natural disasters, such as a flooding rain event, my days can be unpredictable and reactive to the event that has occurred.

Q: What do you like most about your job?

A: The most satisfying part of my job is when something I have designed is constructed properly and providing a solution to someone's problem, such as a drainage or flooding issue.

Q: What do you like least about your job?

A: Sometimes being an engineer can weigh heavy on your mind. It is not a career to enter into without heart. Public safety and welfare is the most important part of being an engineer. Every design has to be created with safety at the forefront. In my discipline of site engineering, storm water and roadway design can threaten the livelihood of people if not done properly. Although this is a stressful part of the job, I believe this stress helps one to be a better engineer.

Q: What personal qualities do you find most valuable for this type of engineering work?

A: Strong self-confidence, excellent communication and social skills along with "thick skin" are qualities I find most valuable for engineering. You will be consistently questioned and challenged, but if you have done your job well you must have the confidence to stand by it and make sure it is implemented properly.

Q: What is the best way to prepare for this type of engineering job?

A: Becoming a professional engineer (PE) first requires a degree in engineering from an accredited university. For civil engineers, the Fundamentals of Engineering exam must be taken and passed soon after graduation. After four years of working under a PE, an engineer can then apply and take the professional engineering exam in their region. If a passing grade is achieved, the engineer will be certified and given the title of PE. Each year or every other year, the PE is required to obtain continuing education units (CEUs) or professional development hours (PDHs) to maintain their licensure. CEUs and PDHs can include online courses, in-person classes, written materials that include a test at the end, seminars, training at conferences, and that sort of thing. This ongoing education and professional development is to help make sure you keep up with changing rules and standards in your field and to help you learn new skills or see how technology is changing the way you are doing things currently.

Q: What other advice do you have for students who might be interested in a career as a civil engineer?

A: Becoming an engineer can be a very rewarding yet demanding career. It is one to be taken very seriously. As a woman engineer, the opportunity is an honor and a challenge. Women engineers have to work even harder to prove they deserve a place in this field and unfortunately have a very tough time being treated with respect. However, when you have a great team of colleagues and peers who support you and know the quality of your work, you feel even more motivated to power on and pave the way for future engineers.

SOURCE NOTES

Introduction: Building the World We Live In

1. Quoted in Charlotte Thomas, "Civil Engineering: Job Hunting," *Graduating Engineer and Computer Careers*. www.graduating engineer.com.

Chapter 1: What Does a Civil Engineer Do?

2. Quoted in Bel Walpole, "ASCE Salary Survey Results Reveal a Civil Engineering Industry in Demand," American Society of Civil Engineers, November 13, 2017. www.news.asce.org.

3. Quoted in OMNNI Associates, "Responsibilities of an OMNNI Associates Construction Projects Leader," 2017. www.omnni .com.

4. Quoted in Rigzone Staff, "What Does It Take to Become an Environmental Engineer?," Rigzone, October 25, 2017. www .rigzone.com.

5. Quoted in Engineering.com, "Materials Engineering Takes a Combination of Technical and Business Skills," June 14, 2013. www.engineering.com.

6. Quoted in Linda Thomas Terhune, "A Transportation Engineer's Quest to Improve Global Planning," Purdue University Engineering Impact, 2017. www.engineering.purdue.edu.

7. Quoted in College Foundation of North Carolina, "Marine Engineer: Interviews." www1.cfnc.org.

8. Quoted in Nick Baveystock, "So What Does a Civil Engineer Do, Exactly?," *Guardian* (Manchester, UK), August 8, 2013. www .theguardian.com.

Chapter 2: How Do You Become a Civil Engineer?

9. Quoted in Doug Scott, "In Its First Year, Civil Engineering Clubs a Clear-Cut Success," ASCE News, November 19, 2013. www.asce.org.

10. Quoted in MIT Civil and Environmental Engineering, "Welcome to Course 1." www.cee.mit.edu.

11. Quoted in Annie Cassutt, "Steel Bridge Aims to Make Nationals at Next Competition," *Iowa State Daily*, November 19, 2017. www.iowastatedaily.com.

12. Quoted in EngineerJobs.com, "So You Want to Be a Civil Engineer," February 13, 2013. https://magazine.engineerjobs .com.

13. Quoted in Cornell Civil and Environmental Engineering, "Spotlight on Students: Morgan Mills." www.cee.cornell.edu.

Chapter 3: What Skills and Personal Qualities Matter Most—and Why?

14. Quoted in EngineerGirl, "Ask an Engineer: Math and Drawing in Civil Engineering," April 26, 2016. www.engineergirl.org.

15. Quoted in Georgia Tech School of Civil and Environmental Engineering, "In Fall Hyatt Lecture, Montanye Says Relationships, Curiosity, Business Skills Key to a Fulfilling Engineering Career," September 20, 2016. www.ce.gatech.edu.

16. Quoted in Stanford Engineering, "Laura Marino," November 2016. www.engineering.stanford.edu.

17. Quoted in Elizabeth Hernandez, "What Does an Engineer Look Like? CU Boulder Campaign Counters Stereotypes," *Daily Camera*, July 4, 2017. www.dailycamera.com.

18. Quoted in Construction Engineering and Management News, "Undergraduate Researches Construction on Mars," Purdue University. www.engineering.purdue.edu.

19. Quoted in Ohio State University Engineering Career Services, "Civil Engineering Success Stories." www.ecs.osu.edu.

20. Quoted in Ohio State University Engineering Career Services, "Civil Engineering Success Stories."

21. Quoted in Ohio State University Engineering Career Services, "Civil Engineering Success Stories."

22. Quoted in Ohio State University Engineering Career Services, "Civil Engineering Success Stories."

Chapter 4: What Is It Like to Work as a Civil Engineer?

23. Quoted in Baveystock, "So What Does a Civil Engineer Do, Exactly?"

24. Quoted in *Building Big*, "Who Builds Big? Patricia Frayre Builds Structures from the Ground Up!," PBS. www.pbs.org.

25. Quoted in Louisa Peacock, "London Olympics 2012: Opening Ceremony to 'Reinvigorate Careers in Engineering," *Telegraph* (London), August 8, 2013. www.telegraph.co.uk.

26. Quoted in *Building Big*, "Who Builds Big?"

Chapter 5: Advancement and Other Job Opportunities

27. Quoted in Georgia Tech College of Engineering, "Should Engineers Get an MBA Degree?," September 28, 2010. www.coe.gatech.edu.

28. Quoted in Ohio State University Engineering Career Services, "Civil Engineering Success Stories."

29. Quoted in Georgina Crouth, "One on One with Georgie: A Natural Candidate to Engineer a Big Difference," *Business Report* (Cape Town, South Africa), December 6, 2017. www.iol.co.za.

30. Quoted in Ohio State University Engineering Career Services, "Civil Engineering Success Stories."

31. Quoted in Kevin Wilcox, "Burned Bridge Offers Clues to Howe Truss Behavior," *Civil Engineering*, February 24, 2015. www.asce.org.

Chapter 6: What Does the Future Hold for Civil Engineers?

32. M. Zanona, "U.S. Infrastructure Report Card: D+," *Hill* (Washington, DC), March 8, 2017. www.thehill.com.

33. Quoted in *Civil + Structural Engineer*, "Getting a Piece of the Renewable Energy Market," January 29, 2014. www.csengineermag.com.

34. Quoted in Construction Engineering and Management News, "Undergraduate Researches Construction on Mars."

35. Quoted in Civil and Environmental Engineering, "High-Speed Rail a New Focus for Railroad Program," University of Illinois at Urbana-Champaign, March 16, 2010. https://cee.illinois.edu.

36. Quoted in Margo Cole, "Breaking the Mould," New Civil Engineer, September 2016. www.newcivilengineer.com.

37. Quoted in Simon Barney, "BBC's MasterChef to Serve Up ICE 200 Celebratory Dinner," Institution of Civil Engineers, December 4, 2017. www.ice.org.uk.

FIND OUT MORE

American Society of Civil Engineers (ASCE)
1801 Alexander Bell Dr.
Reston, VA 20191
www.asce.org

The ASCE is the oldest civil engineering society in the United States. It provides support and training for engineers as well as information and guidance for students who want to become engineers. The ASCE sponsors high school civil engineering clubs by providing mentors and other support for students. The ASCE is also involved with civil engineering competitions for high school and college students.

Institution of Civil Engineers (ICE)
1 Great George St.
Westminster, London
SW1P 3AA
United Kingdom
www.ice.org.uk

ICE is an international organization that supports civil engineering education and the ongoing training and professional development of current engineers. Students can join ICE for free and get advice, learning materials, and the ability to interact with ICE's student network.

TryEngineering
www.tryengineering.org

TryEngineering is an online resource for students who want to learn more about civil engineering and all other engineering disciplines. Students can get advice about what classes to take, what the career is all about, and how to get involved with competitions and other young people who share an interest in engineering. Students can also get information about different universities and the engineering programs they offer.

US Department of Labor

Bureau of Labor Statistics
Postal Square Bldg.
2 Massachusetts Ave. NE
Washington, DC 20212-0001
www.bls.gov

The Bureau of Labor Statistics provides information on a variety of career fields, including civil engineering. Visitors to its website can learn about what civil engineers do and what their working conditions are like. The site also includes information about how to become a civil engineer and what the job prospects are like in every state. You can also learn how the job of civil engineer compares to similar occupations.

INDEX

PICTURE CREDITS

Cover: Thinkstock Images/iStock

6: Maury Aaseng

13: Drazen/iStockphoto.com

20: Goodluz/Depositphotos

26: JayLazarin/iStockphoto.com

34: GaudiLab/Depositphotos

45: NASA/JPL

ABOUT THE AUTHOR

James Roland started out as a newspaper reporter more than twenty-five years ago. He then moved on to become an editor, magazine writer, and author.